THE
PRECISION
HANDCUTTING
OF DOVETAILS

With a Sequence to the Author's
Fifty Years a Planemaker and User

Cecil E. Pierce

With fifty-eight pertinent photos by the author

The Monmouth Press

Monmouth, Maine

ISBN 0-9628001-4-7
Library of Congress Catalog Card Number
95-76717

Published by the Monmouth Press
Monmouth, Maine
Manufactured in the United States of America
First Printing

Dedication

To Lucy, a wife who meant so much,
but is now gone these twenty years,
again I dedicate another book.

Acknowledgements

I am indebted to Eben Blaney, a college student majoring in journalism, whom I hired to rephrase, punctuate and computerize my pages of nearly indecipherable handwriting.

I am also indebted to Arthur Griffiths and his daughter Linda Griffiths of The Monmouth Press. They took it on from there.

Preface

Dovetail joints can be hand-cut with a precision that makes the trial fitting and paring of the joints superfluous. Further paring may even be detrimental to the process. These joints are so precise that the parts need only be "buttered" with adhesive before embracing each other forever. With the dovetail, man has created the strongest joint in woodworking: a creation of beauty, and a source of satisfaction to its creator.

The "modus operandi" used to achieve this, in photos and in prose, is what this book is all about.

Foreword

In this age of automatic machines and fast foods most of us, me included, enjoy the fruits of the technology that produced those machines and those "ready-to-eat" fast foods. Some of us have not allowed the fast and pre-prepared foods to dominate our diets. The flood of fast foods has, to the contrary, heightened our enjoyment of "hand-cooking." So, by the same measure, why should we allow power tools to do it all when "hand-making" in the woodworking shop allows so much versatility and satisfaction? The personal benefit of handwork is the great enjoyment felt by the creator in his or her shop.

At one time I made bamboo fly rods (fishing rods). These were made by precisely hand-planing strips of bamboo which were then glued together to make a hexagonal shaft. This is one of the few areas where the craftsman in wood uses the machinist's ever-present micrometer to measure his work in thousandths of an inch. Another worker in wood who often turns to the micrometer is the pattern-maker.

As you read and work your way through this book you will find me, an ex-machinist, working and talking in thousandths of an inch as I strive towards precision in woodworking.

It is my hope that readers of this book will acquire from it a greater sense and appreciation of the precision I speak of and are able to put such precision to work in woodworking, namely in the process of dovetailing. It is, after all, this effort towards precision in hand-woodworking that bears the fruits which oftentimes become lost in the flood of today's technology.

The Ten Commandments of Precision Dovetailing

I.   Rip all materials to the exact same widths assuming a rectangular or square structure. If a taper is involved, modify as needed.

II.   Cut or otherwise work all ends of the material to be used absolutely square with their faces and edges.

III.   Lay out (physically on floor or bench) all the components and mark on the outside and top edge of each what their assembly status will be, 1-2-3-4. This will leave no doubt later as to which edges will be at the top of the structure, which faces will be on the outside of it, and which ends will be joined together.

IV.   Do all the layout work from the outside. Two exceptions will be noted as we come to them.

V.   All chiseling and paring should be done from the outside (face side) so far as it is possible.

VI.   Always lay out and cut the tails first. They are the patterns for the layout of the pins.

VII.   Disregard the pencil as a layout tool, for it is extremely inaccurate. Also disregard knives and scriber points for the same reason.

VIII.   Very sharp tools are a necessity.

IX.   Always lay out and cut both the pins and tails ⅟₁₆" longer than the thickness of the material being used.

X.   Never allow any tool to leave its imprint below or beyond the baseline.

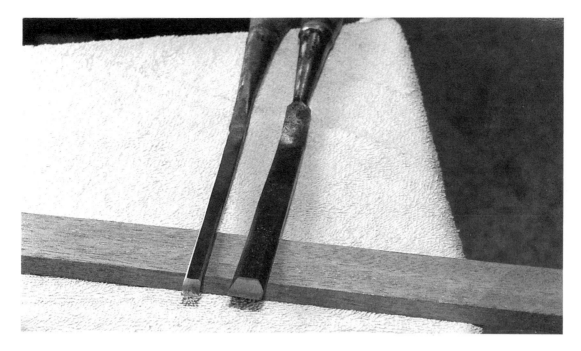

8

Here to the left are two paring chisels, commonly called crank-handle or pattern-maker's chisels. You can, of course, pare your tails and pins with any chisel, but these bent chisels have an undescribable feeling as you slice thousandths-thin shavings with them. I modified these chisels — one is a T. H. Weatherby, the smaller one a Buck Bros. cast steel. There are none better. Their edges are ground very thin. The hollow ground bevel measures, from heel to edge, 18°. The working edge is diamond honed, making it awesomely sharp; they slice pine and mahogany like butter.

I modified these straight chisels by clamping most of their flat length in a vise. Then, with an acetylene torch, I heated the handle part next to the vise until it was at a red heat, and, with a hammer, bent the chisel's handle an estimated ten to fifteen degrees. After the chisel cooled, I reheated it beyond the first heat, and then bent it about one-half the distance opposite the first bend, towards its original position. The vise absorbed any heat which would otherwise have traveled to the cutting edge.

The two short chisels are what I term "chopping-out" chisels. One is Buck Bros. cast steel and the other Charles Buck cast steel. If there are any more sought-after old tools than Buck cast steel, I haven't heard of them.

When chopping out using short chisels you have the advantages of being able to find the line more easily and not having to raise the mallet as high before striking the chisel. The bevels are ground to 22° and, of course, diamond honed. This is about as thin an edge possible that can still stand being driven by a mallet.

These three small steel squares are about all that is needed to cut dovetails in work up to 2" thick. I have cut dovetails in thicknesses from ⅛" to 4", so these will obviously not cover the full spectrum of dovetail possibilities, but they will serve nicely for most.

The square with the narrow blade is very useful and necessary in some work. I modified this from a low-cost engineer's square listed in most tool catalogs. After placing the square in a vise, I hacksawed the top at an angle which made it obvious that that part of it is unusable as a square. The inner angle remains unchanged.

All methods of hand-producing dovetails must have a baseline or its equivalent from which to lay out and then cut the tails and pins. My recommended method is to use a marking gauge — an ancient tool used to cut a fine line accurately for depth and location.

Twenty years ago I probably would not have recommended the above, because the marking gauge's accuracy depends on a square cut on the end of the workpiece, both across the material's width and through its thickness. But today, with power tools such as table saws with miter gauges and the newer chop saws, one or both are found in most shops. Square-ended material is no problem: in fact it is the norm.

What would I have said back then about how to establish a straight, square baseline? Probably I would have suggested the clamped-on straightedge which I used to use. To its credit, the straightedge left no scored line which must be cleaned away later, as with the marking gauge. But the straightedge had its problems, one very disturbing problem being that the wedging action of the chisel would tend to push the straightedge off its intended location.

So here we are going with the marking gauge. But not just any marking gauge: a tuned-up and accurate one.

The marking gauge's inserted tool, shown here, has a "V" profile on its working end. This "V" has a bevel ground on each sloping face, much like a chisel's bevel. It should be honed after grinding so that it has a very sharp edge.

When this cutting tool is inserted in the beam of the marking gauge, it is done so with the bevel facing the fence of the marking gauge. As the tool is drawn across the work this bevel wants to sheer off course but the fence, tight against the end of the material being used, will not allow it to do so.

Therefore, the baseline produced is precisely parallel to the squared end of the workpiece.

← This is a common hand plane — it could be either wood or iron — the iron of which I have modified with a small hand grinder. Used for quickly and easily cutting down of the endwood and glue preparatory to finishing any dovetail project. The edge ends up being a series of small gouges which cut effortlessly.

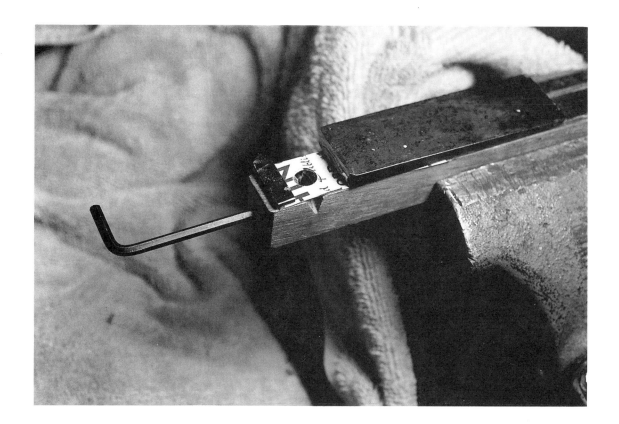

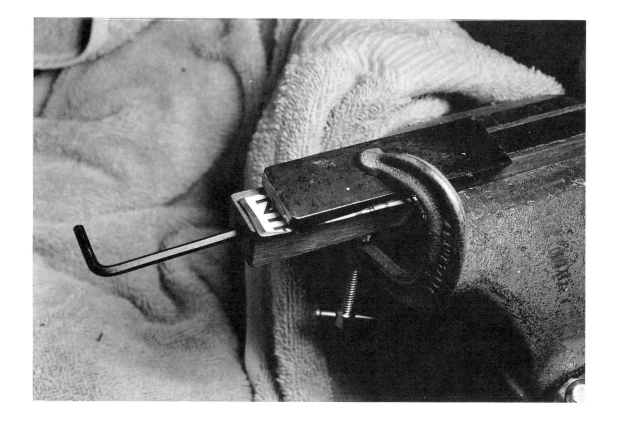

When scoring a track for the baseline with the marking gauge, there is no need to make it any deeper than .006". Anything deeper than this is difficult to remove completely. For my own work I use .004" for a scoring depth. Finding the scored mark, which seems like only a faint line, is easy with the edge of a sharp chisel. Hold the chisel in a vertical position beyond the scribed baseline in front of you and begin drawing it towards you, letting the chisel's edge lightly drag on the work surface. When the chisel reaches the line you can both feel and hear it falling into the track. That's for .004": if your scribe line is .006" deep, finding it will be more like stubbing your toe on a spruce root while walking through the woods.

How do we accurately produce a line this deep with no way of measuring its depth? Here, step by step, is what I believe to be the only way.

Strip the fence off the beam of the marking gauge and put it aside. Place the beam in a vise horizontally, with the working side up and the scoring end out by the edge of the vise an inch or so. Now cut three strips of newsprint — newsprint is a strong .002" if you take it from the *Wall Street Journal* or the *Boothbay Register*. Cut the pieces two or three inches long by the width of the beam. Now, with a paper punch, or by other means, cut a small hole in each piece of paper quite near one end. Place these holes over the cutter hole in the beam. Now place any small piece of smooth iron over the paper and hole. Lightly clamp it to the beam. Next, put the cutter in place; bevel toward the fence. Hold the sharp point against the flat iron with one hand while tightening the cutter-holding mechanism with the other. Remove the sandwich of paper and iron to find the cutter protruding the proper distance out of the beam.

To make the previously described precision adjustment, it will likely be necessary to modify the marker's cutter-holding mechanism thusly: Bore and tap the wood in the end of the marking-gauge beam through to the cutter for a ¼" x 20 U.S.S. Allen head set screw. This must be done with a gun tap (no relation to the shooting kind). I believe the catalogs call them "spiral-pointed." By either name, this type of tap is what is needed to cut a successful thread in wood. Your hole will want to be drilled with a #7 drill.

To perform this operation, clamp the beam vertically in a vise on the drill press. Bore the #7 hole. Remove the bit from the chuck and replace it with the tap. Turn the tap in by hand-working the drive belt. This will produce a nice thread.

Assuming that you now have a properly cut baseline, we should begin laying out the tails from it. This may be done in two ways. The first way is from a pattern like those shown to the left. These patterns of ⅛" birch plywood are fast to use and versatile. From these few patterns I am able to lay out most of my dovetail work.

The second method is to individually lay out each bevel using a bevel tool, as shown below left, and a sharp pencil. Whether marking the tail layout from a pattern or with use of a bevel tool, this is the last and only time that the pencil is used as a marking instrument in the layout process.

Perhaps this is a good place to say something about the bevel angle. Much has been written about this, mostly in terms of ratio like 4:1 or 5:1, with the idea that the ratio should change according to whether the material used is hardwood or softwood. I don't get very excited about all of this. My bevel is locked and pinned at 9° for all woods. It could just as well be 8° or 10° for all that it matters.

However you do it, make sure that the half tails, at the top and bottom of each joint, are at least half the width of the full tails. Otherwise the narrow wood will likely crack away during assembly.

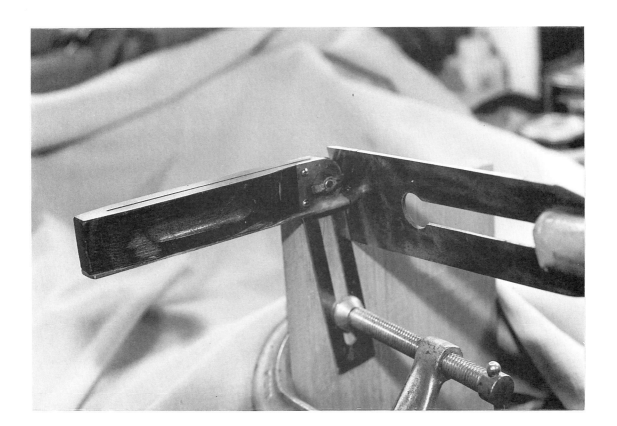

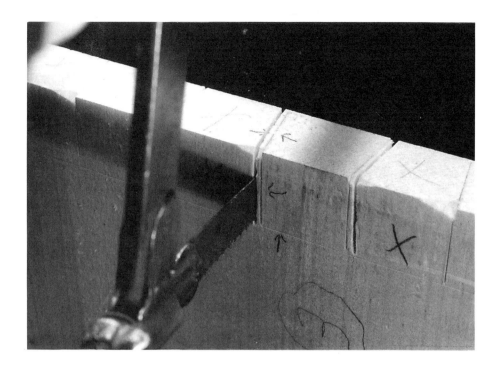

awing down the tails is the next operation. It takes a certain kind of courage for me to tell you that I put away my three nice dovetail saws in favor of a cast-off hacksaw frame with a fourteen-tooth hacksaw blade. There are several reasons for this. First, dovetail saws do not cut fast or well. Second, they are impossible to steer. In addition, their small teeth are difficult to sharpen.

The hacksaw blade is the antithesis of all this. The blade's perfectly formed teeth of high-speed steel will probably last a lifetime before needing to be replaced. The steering ability alone makes the blade the ultimate selection. The hacksaw's great steering capability is further enhanced after I grind the back of the blade away until it is only one-half of its original width. This latter modification came too late for the photo, which shows the blade at full width.

The picture attests to the hacksaw blade's superior cutting ability and demonstrates the proper way to saw down. About ⅟₁₆" is left on the waste side of the lay-out iron's score mark. This will be pared away after chopping out the waste pieces, which are marked with an "X" in both photos. Notice how the blade is down to but not over the baseline. If the saw blade is allowed to go below the baseline, the resulting overcut will become filled with glue when assembled and show later as an ugly black line in the finished product.

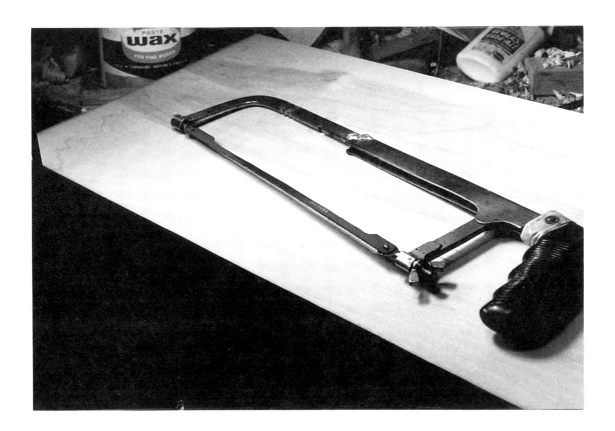

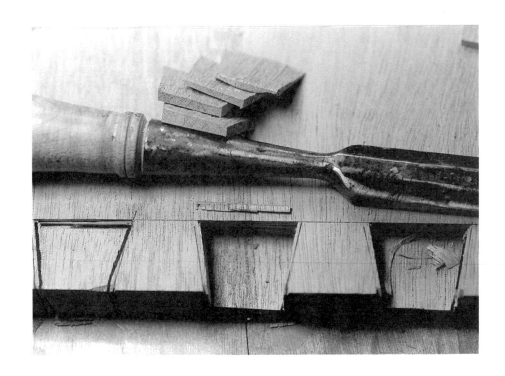

The next step is "chopping out the waste." Some may see this as a difficult process. What a field day some dovetailers have when writing for the woodworking magazines — they enjoy explaining their "easy" methods used to take out the waste from between the pins and tails. Most would have the reader put a small coping saw down the existing saw kerf, then turn it at a right angle and saw across to the other kerf, proud of the baseline. This allows the waste to fall out in one piece. What is not explained is that, after this, one still has to chisel down the end wood to remove that which is left on.

My method goes like this: The wood you are dovetailing is dogged down to the bench with the out or "good" side up and the end to be worked facing you. For tools one needs only a chisel and mallet. The chisel should be a bit wider than one-half the width of the waste to be chopped out. The round lignum vitae is an excellent choice in a mallet.

I believe it was Ted Williams who said, "To hit a round ball with a round bat is the most difficult thing to do in sports." I often think of this when using the round mallet, though I have never managed to miss the chisel handle with it. I prefer the round mallet because it is less bulky and it feels better to me.

A chisel is a wedge, so when it is driven into wood there has to be a reaction. This problem needs to be recognized whenever wood is to be chiseled accurately. We have a baseline which we have gone to considerable lengths to establish accurately. Careless chiseling may accidentally move it. With the chisel held vertically, its bevel towards the waste wood, strike the chisel with the mallet lightly, letting the mallet's weight drop from a height of about 4". The chisel will penetrate perhaps .010". The baseline was cut .006" deep, so the chisel is now down about .016" to ¹⁄₁₆". Now, with the chisel held low and in front of the vertical cut, cut out the chip shown in front of the chisel in the picture (opposite). The chip in the left-hand pin has not been taken out yet. At this point, hit the vertical cut hard with one blow of the chisel, then split out the resulting chip. As you can see, four easy lifts have been taken out and the cut is halfway through.

When all the pins on that side are down halfway, the workpiece is turned over and the same treatment is given on the backside, with one exception: with the chisel in the baseline, as before, we strike a *strong* blow this first time. The strength of the blow will set the baseline back slightly, thus ensuring that the finished joint will be a tight fit on the outside face when assembled. The upper picture is of the pins getting the described treatment.

19

The tails are "chopped out." It is now time to begin the crucial and precise paring of the waste to the scored lines of the tails. To begin, clamp the workpiece vertically in the vise with the outside facing you.

Your chisel must be sharp, sharp, sharp! — capable of paring a paper-thin shaving when necessary. Also, it must be remembered that the scoring tool's lines are sacred; they must not be altered by any paring that is done. These two basic requirements go hand in hand in accurate, successful paring.

You will find that this paring across the grain is liable to split off the back edge, especially if you're working with mahogany. To eliminate this, use a skewing up-and-down motion as you work deeper with your chisel.

When finished with this procedure, the back line of the tail's pared side must be square with the front scored line for its entire length, from baseline to endwood. That is, the backside of the tails should be a mirror image of the front. This is accomplished by "pare-and-try" — paring until the little square, held horizontally with its beam resting on the back of the tail, shows the back edge to be square and parallel with the untouched front tail scoring.

After this has been accomplished, carefully "back out" the area between the front and back edges of the tail. This is to further ensure a good fit when the joint is assembled. Be careful, though, not to do so too close to the top scoring, as you run the danger of damaging this untouchable score. Also, make certain that the lower corner, front and back, are cleaned out, otherwise some small, unfinished corner might not allow the final, close fit at the baseline when the joint is assembled.

I will try to explain the reason, now, for all this accuracy in paring the tails. That back edge, which has been so carefully established, is going to be the pattern for the scoring of the pins. Understand? If not, you are about to see.

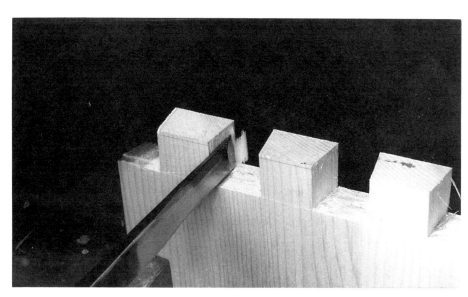

← Here the paring chisel is paring off a .002"-thick shaving. If your chisel will not do this, it is not sharp enough for accurate results.

21

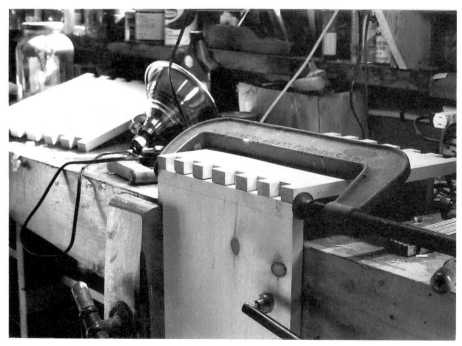

Laying out the pins from the tails is next, assuming ordinary sized projects. To begin this stage of the process, put the pin wood in the vise vertically at a convenient height above the bench (2" or 3"). Make sure that the end to be marked is up and the good side is out. Next, lay the corresponding tails piece on top of the end wood of the upright workpiece so that the tails are directly over the future site of their mating pins and the length of the workpiece extends over the bench. Block up the end of the tailpiece until the two workpieces are perpendicular.

Next, put a clamp across the two pieces in such a manner that it holds them in their relative positions. I am relying on my pictures to better detail all of this. Viewed vertically from above, the chopped-out and pared tailwood, at the baseline of the tails, should just "touch on" the inside of the pin wood. To achieve this, tap the tailwood with a hammer after clamping. When all is in proper relation the tails should be out by the pin wood the $\frac{1}{16}$" that was allowed from the original baseline scribing.

Score the lines for the pins using the scoring tool. The bevel of the tool should be on the pin side of the score, with the flat side against the tails of the top piece. When scoring, lay the scoring tool back from vertical a few degrees to ensure an accurate score tight to the base of the tail which you are tracing. Again, study the photos.

Continue until all pins are scored. After unclamping the setup, it is a good idea to mark all the wastewood with an "X" for insurance that later the work will not be ruined by starting to saw down on the wrong side of the line.

← Laying out the pins using 4" thick material.

23

In this photo the pins have already had their location and top bevel laid out on the endwood from their mating tails. Here, the pins are being squared down to the baseline. The procedure for doing this is as follows.

First, a wood straightedge is clamped to the workpiece precisely on the baseline. Then, on top of the straightedge, as in the picture, an adjustable square blade is clamped on, using its square end for a convenient marking gauge. The square's blade is moved and reclamped along the work, in line with each pin's scoring on the endwood of the workpiece. As in the previous marking-down of the tails, each of these lines must be an accurate continuation of the top line.

After the pins are marked, clear away all the straightedges and clamps. Then, deepen the top and vertical scores by freehand. Deepen the latter at the angle dictated by the bevel of the top scoring. In doing all of this, keep turning the scoring tool so that the bevel of its edge is towards the waste wood during each scoring. This will give a sharp and perpendicular line to pare to.

In deepening each scoring, one must use considerable judgment and restraint. As noted previously, the chisel blade is a wedge; it is bound to react as it penetrates a piece of wood. One result of this reaction is the displacement of a line from its original location which is, of course, unacceptable.

← Nice fitting joint ready to be glued and then cut down level with the parent material.

Now there is a set of pins laid out to accurately fill the spaces between the tails. Next we "saw down" and "chop out" the waste between the pins exactly as we did with the tails. The paring of the pins, however, will go faster and easier than the paring of the tails. Only the deepened score lines are, again, sacred.

Remember, when paring the tails, the need for keeping the back edge, or "in" side of your workpiece's tails, square and parallel with those sacred, scored marks of your tail layout on the front or "out" side of your workpiece? This was done so that the mating pins could be laid out accurately from the backside of the tails. Well, we don't give a damn about the back line of the pins, just so long as it is not out by the front line in relation to the pins bevel, as laid out on the endwood. If this were the case, the joint would not assemble.

Because the pins are beveled through the workpiece's thickness, the way to check this back line is by using the little square with its beam on top of the pin, and note if the back line needs more paring to be square with the endwood's score. Again, it is better to pare beyond square, below that sacred score, to ensure the joint's fit.

← Laying out the big four-inch Douglas fir tails.

27

I may have to rely on the photos to help me explain the modus operandi for the cutting-out of the half-pins. So please take the opportunity to study them as I describe the process. Here it is.

First, with the nice, sharp chisel you are using, outline the baseline on three sides. Do this very lightly, just as you did when taking out the first small chip from the wastewood before chopping out.

I was derelict way back when I explained the marking of the baseline in not saying that the baseline should be established across the edge of the material used for the pins as well as across the face of that material.

Back to the half-pins. After the three scores are carefully chiseled and the piece of wastewood is chopped or sawed away, undercut the area between the three chiseled lines (note the inked area in the photo) with a small chisel or gouge. This ensures that the tailwood will be a nice, tight fit.

Also note in the photo the small chamfer on the upper edge of the pins. This allows assembly without the sharp edges "digging in."

Two-inch-thick master corner.

Three-inch-thick master corner.

We are nearing the end of the trail. Four corners cut, pared, and all a proven fit. The mallet, chisels, saw, and marking gauge are all laid aside. Now to assemble the fruits of our labors. Up to this time you have been submitted to new and unusual — even groundbreaking — methods of procedure. Allow me to continue in the same manner as I share with you my original approach and techniques for precision assembly of the material.

One spring I made 18 so-called sea chests pictured elsewhere. This involved 73 linear feet of dovetails, all fitted with precision as cut!

I had already decided that four corners swathed in glue were too much to assemble all at one time. So I decided to glue up only one and let it cure before adding the other three sides. But even that first corner alone gave me a terrible time. My squares, and clamps, not to mention my hands, were covered with glue. There had to be a better way. I allowed ample time to consider the problem.

I determined that what was needed was that which I will name a "master corner" — one whose precision and strength would be like Caesar's wife: above suspicion. (I love that little bit of wisdom, even though shady and not mine originally. I borrowed it from Fred Hodgson, who wrote woodworking books some seventy-five years ago. As a youth I ate them up. I used Hodgson's expression in my first book and will probably use it in book #3, if and when.)

Back to the subject. I set about constructing this "master corner," pictured at the left, from 3" thick, thoroughly dried, maple. It is dovetailed and set in epoxy resin. After having cured, it was handworked carefully until square in all directions.

It has proved itself consistent at producing perfectly square corners in all my projects, and its versatility surpassed all expectations. I used it to start assembly not only in the small box made of ⅛" thick material, but also in assembly of the 4" thick, Douglas fir coffee table!

I strongly recommend that you make a "master corner," and it need not be as thick as 3". One of any 1" hard wood would be sufficient. The sides are 12" long by 8" wide. To use it, thoroughly coat it with any furniture wax. Then lightly clamp the workpieces to it, driving and clamping the joints together. Cure for twenty-four hours, then add the three other joints to the first one. The parts all having been cut to the same lengths respectively, squareness comes automatically to the project, thanks to that first, perfectly square corner.

With all the previous operations completed, there are four corners of a box, chest, or whatever you are making, covered with a mess of cured glue and excessive endwood. You might quickly think it can be removed with a belt sander, but it cannot; if for no other reason, the sanding belt will clog up with glue. But there are other reasons. Did you ever try to sand a piece of pine with a knot in it? A pine knot is endwood and the sander will not take it down nearly as fast as the surrounding wood.

I know of no other way to do this than with a sharp hand plane adjusted for a .002" to .003" shaving. Work from both edges inward to avoid split-off from the far edge. Also, skew the plane when possible. Finish the smoothing with a turned-edge scraper.

In this photo the Nikon has captured not only the laying-out methods herein described, but the growth rings of the wood, recording forever that it took the soil of British Columbia (or was it Washington or Oregon? We'll never know), nurtured by the warm atmosphere blowing in from the Pacific, thirty-two years to grow four inches, in thickness, of this fabulously strong and rot-resistant Douglas fir, so sought after world wide for shipbuilding and wherever wooden bridges and piers are still built.

If further proof of the wood's resistance to the ravages of rot and deterioration is needed, one has only to view the old sailing-ship hulks — built of this wood in the World War One era — lying at the shoreline in Wiscasset, Maine. Their masts are still standing. Nature is having a hard time destroying (recycling?) them!

Small wonder that this marine contractor commissioned this piece of furniture to be made of the material which is more or less his stock in trade.

Did anyone ever see dovetailed furniture four inches thick before? One of a kind?

If I never drive a chisel into Douglas fir again, it will be soon enough. It also has a great resistance to hand tools!

As an afterthought, I believe the wood of this table is on its second mission. That black streak of stain could only have been caused by the leaching of iron fastenings from its previous use!

32

Dovetailing graces a four-inch-thick Douglas fir coffee table.

A pair of mahogany dovetailed chests. My forebears, being seafaring men, carried these to sea with them to hold spare clothing and any other spare materials. They are three feet long and thirteen inches high and wide.

A dovetailed walnut and bird's-eye maple chairside stand.

Two-inch-thick mahogany dovetails in the author's living room.

Perhaps the strongest way to create a table top-leg marriage is to screw and glue the leg to the inside corner of the dovetailed skirt board. In addition to its great strength it is beautiful.

A collector's ransom of old and restored large chisels, and of course some dovetails.

Another dovetailed sea chest, this time white pine.

A replica of a two-man 46-inch-long x 5" wide Swiss plane, made in 1613.

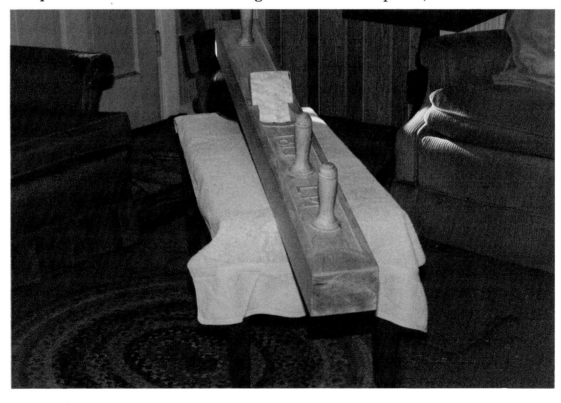

SEQUENCE

TO

FIFTY YEARS A PLANEMAKER

AND USER

Since writing *Fifty Years a Planemaker* I have made a very important discovery relative to the precision adjustment of the iron, both vertically and laterally, in any hand plane. This adjustment is so simple that it is unbelievable that someone else has not done it in the thousands of years since planes were first developed.

With this system the adjustment of the plane iron is simple and infinite, unlike the adjustment system of iron planes with their inaccurate, loose, and sloppy threads for their vertical mechanisms, and their inadequate lateral movement. The simple modifications I speak of allow the hand plane to graduate into the precision hand tool category. In photos and in prose, here is how it is done to any plane.

The holes for the screws are drilled and tapped under the drill press, using the same size and equipment as outlined for the cutter of the marking gauge. I used a smaller screw size, ¹⁰⁄₃₂, for the little 60½ Stanley block plane pictured.

With these side screws the lateral adjustment can be held to thousandths of an inch. Not only that, but the plane iron will stay as adjusted no matter how much it is advanced or retrieved, or even removed and replaced.

Now for the vertical adjustment. It is done with the light striking of a hammer — it has always been so with wooden planes. The iron, however, can not be retrieved under control without my next modification. Before this improvement, when retrieval was necessary, it was done by striking a sharp blow with the hammer on the front top of the plane's body. This brought the iron back for a new start of being tapped ahead — hopefully not too much this time.

My modification solves this retrieval problem. With a small niche ground in the heel of the bevel with a hand grinder, the iron, when necessary, may be precisely retrieved with a small nail set or center punch and hammer. And, with the lateral adjustment screws in place, the iron remains adjusted in that regard throughout any vertical adjustments.

A word of caution. A friend whose advice I value highly suggested that both screws on one side should be backed off slightly because expansion and contraction in wooden hand planes could cause the side wood to crack. This is excellent advice and makes a lot of sense. I do not, however, do it myself, and the many planes of various woods that I use have caused me no trouble.

When Scott Landis, a writer and photographer, came to my shop and home recently to interview me for an article about my planemaking for a woodworking magazine, he brought along a copy of the poster shown opposite. Scott and Silas Kopf, in cooperation with Lee Valley Tools of Ottawa, Ontario, had produced this poster, the sales of which would benefit the W.A.R.P.

To say that Scott got me interested is to put it mildly. I was ecstatic, knowing immediately what I wanted to do and what I would do — make a replica of that big, four-foot-long Swiss jointer pictured in the center of the poster.

Replication went like this: A search of the premises for a piece of dry wood produced a piece of soft maple, 3" thick and 42" long. I needed wood 3¾" thick; gluing a piece of rosewood to the bottom took care of this discrepancy. The shortness I would have to live with.

I don't know, nor do I want to know, how many hours went into that plane by the time all the more or less straightforward woodworking and carving was completed. Even then, I had a plane but no iron for it. So off to the used tool places I went, where I located only one possible candidate — a butcher's cleaver with a hardened and tempered cutting edge. Days later, after cutting up and brazing the old cleaver back together, I had an iron 3½" wide by 7½" long. It was not wide enough, but it would have to do.

It had taken over a week of day and night work on the plane before it produced its first shaving. A few swipes with just me pushing, watching the thick, endless shaving roll out of the top, and I was in love.

But disappointment soon crept in. The plane was 4" too short, and the iron was not just as it should be. I would have to try again.

Another search of the premises, plus an inventory of son Carl's wood pile, produced a kiln-dried plank of 2⅛" x 9" x 8' sugar or rock maple. It would glue up and produce the 4" x 5" x 4' needed for an exact replica.

Some three weeks later the plane was finished. That rock maple was well named — it was hard beyond belief! It took three days just to chip out the opening for the iron! The iron? Oh, yes. This time I sent to Starrett for a piece of tool steel from which I could make a proper iron 3¾" x 7" long. The hardening and tempering were straightforward, allowing me to do it myself. And to this finished replica, I allowed myself the liberty and luxury of installing my adjustment, as outlined previously, in both planes. The worth of the system showed up beautifully in these big planes.

Opposite: Photography by Lee Valley Tools, Ottawa, Ontario, courtesy of WARP (Woodworkers Alliance for Rainforest Protection). This photo has been issued as one of a pair of color posters of historic planes from the Pascal Collection of the Canadian Museum of Civilization/Musée Canadien des Civilisations, Hull, Québec. The set of two 19" x 27" posters may be obtained by sending a check for $22.00 U.S. (postage paid) to: WARP, One Cottage Street, Easthampton, MA 01027.

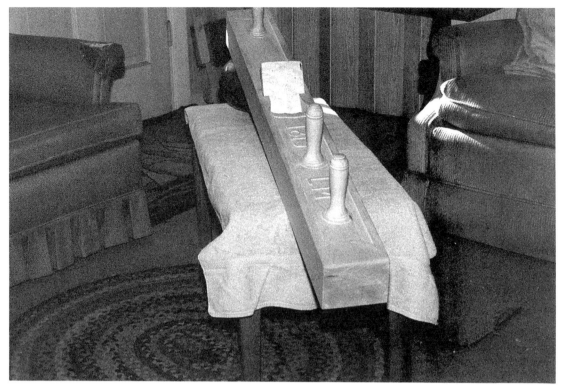

The coffee table under the plane is 3' long.

Three ordinary bench planes — two jacks and a smoother — are dwarfed by the big jointer.

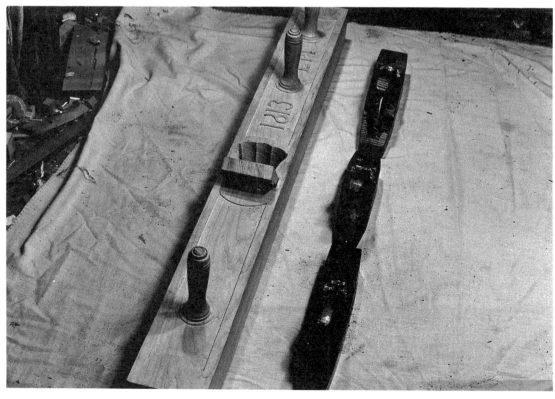

Who used these big two-man planes? There is a dearth of information. I can come up with only two instances in which the planes were used, this first account being only fragmentary and uncertain.

Maurice Sherman remembers a fellow workman, long since expired, telling a lunchtime story of working in a shipyard where he wore a harness attached by rope to a plane which he pulled. That kind of plane and workpiece is lost to time.

I know of at least half a dozen cornice-moulding planes with holes bored through the front end for a helper to pull with a rope lanyard, and this could well have been what Maurice had heard tell of. But I had not heard of any two-man plane for smoothing or jointing until I finished the first plane and took it to friend Jim Stevens, whom I found recovering nicely from surgery.

"Jim, did you ever know or hear of anyone using a two-man plane?" I asked hopefully.

"Yes," Jim replied. "During the last war I was superintendent of a shipyard in Camden [Maine]. We were building wooden cargo vessels. One time we had to make some bollards." Bollards are posts that extend up through the deck of a vessel to make hawsers fast to.

"These were 12" x 12" right from the saw in British Columbia," Jim continued. "There were two of them. They were big and heavy and needed to be planed. It would have taken all hands to put them through the planer." This was fifty years ago, when not every small shipyard had fork lifts.

"I had two Finnish brothers working for me," recalled Jim. "When they heard what I was proposing to do, one of them came to me and said that they would clean up those timbers by hand if I would allow.

"Well, sir," Jim said to me, "they blocked up those timbers to a convenient height and went at it with a two-man plane, one man on the front side and the other on the opposite side, planing diagonally across the grain. They had those two timbers cleaned up in no time."

I am limited to this small amount of information concerning the use of these planes. I am counting on someone who is knowledgeable in this area to help fill me in.

Au revoir.

SUPPLEMENT

Having exhausted all material relative to the cutting of dovetails, only to learn from my publisher that this book doesn't contain the minimum number of pages required to qualify for a copyright, I find myself obliged to carry on in a manner which, though not germane to the title, is hopefully interesting and instructive.

PRELUDE

Next door to my home here in Southport, Maine sits a venerable old house built sometime between the years of 1812 and 1830. It houses the town's historical society. As a neighbor and a member of the board of directors I contribute to this society in all ways possible.

At a recent board meeting it was voted that the existing building be enlarged by the addition of an "L." It was further decided that this new wing should, so far as reasonably possible, architecturally and in detail, appear to have been built at the same period as the original house. The requirement of an outside door for entrance and exit posed an immediate problem — any new, factory-made door would suggest, at a glance, the recent construction of the building. Realizing this, I volunteered to replicate in design and construction the beautiful six-panel, white pine, hand-made original front door which, after about one hundred and sixty years of Maine's on-again and off-again weather, was still in excellent condition.

I would, by hand work, make the ten through-and-pinned mortise and tenons but would stop short of ripping the two-inch plank with a hand saw and hand-planing it, as was done with the original door. Most likely the original door maker had also avoided the ripping and planing. He probably had apprentices to do this drudgery — a system which today seems just short of slavery.

Some of the problems — problems now but "run of the mill" then — and their mastery follows.

Using the mortising chisel to chop down the vertical side of a mortise. With the heavy hammer the chisel can be driven down about ⅜". The chisel's bevel should face in the direction of the length of the mortise. Waste is broken out with force of hammer and leverage.

Mortise and tenon joinery was how furniture and houses were put together before the days of power tools. At about the turn of the century mortising chisels became absent from the listings in tool catalogs. Although I have owned a set of used mortising chisels as a collector, this was the first time that I had put them to use. I was impressed with their practical design and function.

This was a tool designed to be abused. In its proper use the mortising chisel was driven into the wood as far as it could go, using a three-pound hammer. Then, using the hammer on its wooden handle for leverage, the chisel was forced out of the wood, bringing with it great, heavy chips. No holes were first bored. Holes, in fact, would hinder the chisel's function. When the operation was judged to be halfway through, the workpiece was then turned over in the vise and chopped through so that the mortises would meet in the middle. A surprisingly clean and accurate through-mortise was the result.

Note in the photo that the layout was done with a marking tool, leaving a nice scored line to work to.

A close-up of the door's hand-made paneling with hand-made moulding. I did the panel raising with a Stanley #10½ rabbet plane using a guide clamped to the workpiece.

Having completed the hand-mortising and tenoning of the door's stiles and rails, let's digress and turn to the methods I was forced to devise to replicate the hand-made moulding that so nicely set off the raised panels of the door.

To replicate any moulding, start with a contour gauge. A contour gauge is a cluster of steel or plastic leaves that are held loosely together. The leaves can be manipulated to form any curve and thus match the profile of a given moulding. With the use of this tool the contour of the moulding I need is transferred from the moulding to be replicated to the ends of a 2" piece of pine of suitable size and shape. Then, with chisel, gouge and file, this piece of wood is worked out to be a match of the moulding wanted.

Now this curve needs to be transferred to a plane's cutter. The curve that we have made, if laid out directly on the plane's cutter, will not produce the desired profile because the cutter is held at a 45° angle when mounted in the plane. For this reason the dye-coated end of the blank cutter is laid in the simple jig shown and the piece of moulding, with its end cut at 45°, is pushed up to the cutter in order to transfer the proper profile. The moulding is lightly fastened there so that an ice pick or similar tool can accurately scribe the working contour.

With the cutter made we must now find the proper tool to put it in. Being a planemaker I could make a moulded body for it, but for all that I know it would not find any future use beyond the job at hand. Too much effort for so small a gain!

My thinking harks back to a time when I needed to plane the edges of round tables with varying radii. To do this I had purchased an old, #4 Stanley at the local used tool barn for $15. It had a broken handle — they always do — but glue took care of that problem. I discarded all adjusting components save for the lever cap and then drilled four ¼" holes through the sole — one on either side of the front knob and, in back, one on either side of the handle. These holes were to hold and index a "shoe" of whatever radius was desired. The shoes, made from a 2" maple plank, were sawed so they were ¼" thick where the blade extended down through the plane's sole. Because the plane's lateral adjustments had been removed, the side of the plane's shell was drilled and tapped for ¼" x 20 thread, flat head set screws, ¼" long. (The proper drill for ¼" x 20 is #7.) This is something that, as a planemaker, I do to all my planes, whether wooden or metal. It allows for very accurate adjustment.

This plane worked very nicely. Why not make a shoe for it to back up the new molding cutter I had made?

And now for a few words of caution and know-how concerning the working-out of the cutting edge of the cutter. First, treat the scribed line as sacred — it is to be untouched and visible when the edge is finished. Remove the excess metal by whatever means are available, mostly by various grinders. For the final tool to work up to the scribed line I used a small hand grinder tooled with the small, mounted stone which is so commonly used to sharpen the teeth of a chainsaw. Work the edge up to the line square with the face of the tool, then carefully grind away the back bevel. After this, carefully hone both sides of the edge.

The Stanley #55 plane with its multiple cutters and a few adjustable runners has shown that a full-bodied contour in back of the cutter for the plane to rest on wasn't absolutely necessary. So, with this in mind, I'll make a ¼", flat, maple sole for the plane. With clamps to hold it securely, four holes are drilled in the new shoe through the existing holes in the plane's sole. These will accurately index the shoe whenever it is used. For now they hold the shoe in place so that it may be marked and trimmed to the plane's width. The shoe's rectangular slot for the cutter to pass through may be located accurately now as well.

A word of caution here. Plan to have the underside or bevel side of the cutter rest firmly on the wood of the shoe, even if some wood needs to be pared away later. This will ensure that the cutter doesn't chatter when in use.

With the shoe and its cutter firmly in their respective places, glue a 1" x ¼" piece of maple to the shoe, on edge and tightly up against the cutter sidewise. This piece should extend the full length of the plane and protrude down by the cutter ½" or so. This will be the plane's working fence.

My plane is almost ready to be pushed into the business of forming the edge of a pine board into the moulding desired. But there is one more hurdle: moulding planes traditionally have a bottom, through which the cutter protrudes, that is a carbon copy of the cutter's curvature. This would be very difficult and time-consuming to reproduce. However, the Stanley #55 plane with its two adjustable runners tells us, if we choose to listen, that a moulding plane does not necessarily need to have that full body of curves in front of and behind the cutter.

So, with this useful bit of knowledge, I'll glue two ¼" maple strips of proper width, before and behind the cutter. The two behind should be cut at 45° so that they can be pushed up against the cutter to support the cutter and prevent chatter. They should also be hard up against the fence and about ¹⁄₆₄" lower than the cutter ahead of it. The two strips in front should be cut at more than 45° to allow space for the shavings to pass through. The cutter is in the proper position when its lowest curve is a shaving higher than the base surface. Most of the above can be deduced from the photos.

This photo shows the plane in use throwing out a full width shaving from its mouth. A moulding plane doesn't function any better than this! Mine already has three different shoes and cutters for doing special jobs, and more are planned.

See you in the next book, *Sharpening and Honing the Edge with Diamond.*